Rivers

REVISED AND UPDATED

Catherine Chambers and Nicholas Lapthorn

Heinemann
LIBRARY

www.heinemann.co.uk/library
Visit our website to find out more information about Heinemann Library books.

To order:
☎ Phone 44 (0)1865 888066
▤ Send a fax to 44 (0)1865 314091
▱ Visit the Heinemann Library Bookshop at www.heinemann.co.uk/library to browse our catalogue and order online.

Editorial: Joanna Talbot
Design: Richard Parker and Q2A Solutions
Illustrations: Jeff Edwards
Picture Research: Hannah Taylor
Production: Duncan Gilbert

Originated by Chroma Graphics (Overseas) Pte. Ltd
Printed and bound in China by CTPS

ISBN 978 0 431 10991 6 (hardback)
11 10 09 08 07
10 9 8 7 6 5 4 3 2 1

ISBN 978 0 431 11001 1 (paperback)
12 11 10 09 08
10 9 8 7 6 5 4 3 2 1

British Library Cataloguing in Publication Data
Chambers, Catherine, 1954-
 Rivers. - 2nd ed. - (Mapping earthforms)
1. Rivers - Juvenile literature 2. Stream ecology - Juvenile literature
I. Title II. Lapthorn, Nicholas
551.4'83

A full catalogue record for this book is available from the British Library.

Acknowledgements
The publishers would like to thank the following for permission to reproduce photographs: Alamy Images: pp. **7** (Robert Harding Picture Library Ltd), **9** (Sean O'Neill); Bruce Coleman Ltd/A Potts p. **17**; Ecoscene pp. **24** (Gryniewicz), **5** (N Hawkes); Getty Images/Stone p. **4**; Lonely Planet/Oliver Strewe p. **13**; naturepl.com/Dave Watts p. **18**; Oxford Scientific pp. **16** (Geoff Kidd), **19** (Keith Ringland); Photolibrary/Richard Packwood p. **26**; Robert Harding Picture Library pp. **25** (Anthony King), **20** (Charles Bowman); Science Photo Library/M-Sat Ltd p. **10**; Still Pictures pp. **14** (Jorgen Schytte), **23** (Paul Harrison).

Cover photograph reproduced with permission of Photolibrary/Tui De Roy

Every effort has been made to contact copyright holders of any material reproduced in this book. Any omissions will be rectified in subsequent printings if notice is given to the publishers.

Contents

Any words appearing in the text in bold, **like this**, are explained in the Glossary. You can find the answers to Map Active questions on page 29.

What is a river?

A river is a body of flowing water. Sometimes it rushes and rages. At other times it flows slowly along. Rivers always travel downhill, pulled by Earth's **gravity**. They can start from high up in hills or mountains, from lakes, or from lots of little streams joining together to form a river. Most rivers end up flowing into the sea. Think of your favourite river. Can you describe it?

How did rivers begin?

When the first rain fell on Earth thousands of years ago, it began to be affected by gravity. The rain that fell on mountains and hills gathered in dips and cracks. When enough water collected it began to flow downhill in tiny **channels**. As more and more water fell, each channel became bigger and wider to form streams and rivers. Today, Earth's **water cycle** continues to make streams and rivers flow.

▼ The Amazon in Brazil is the second-longest river in the world. It can clearly be seen in this satellite image, running from west to east across Brazil. It runs from the cold Andes Mountains, through hot, **tropical** rainforests and into the Atlantic Ocean.

▲ Plants, animals, and humans cannot live without water. Clean rivers such as this one provide the perfect home for many plants and animals. Polluted rivers have less oxygen in the water and may contain chemicals that harm life in the river.

What do rivers look like?

Rivers begin on high ground as streams, **springs**, or patches of wet ground. As the water gathers it flows downhill. As the river continues to flow downstream towards the sea it gets wider and deeper. Even though the slope of the land gets less, the river still flows quickly. As the river flows into lakes and seas it finally starts to slow down. The strength of the water and the pull of gravity help to carve out shapes in Earth. Rivers change the landscape and are themselves always changing.

Life in and around rivers

Rivers are full of life. Plants grow well in and around rivers. All kinds of animals live in or close to the water. Living things have **adapted** to rivers. Humans could not have survived without rivers, but we have also changed rivers and their landscapes in different parts of the world.

Rivers of the world

The world has millions of rivers and streams. Some rivers are tiny, while others flow a very long way through many countries and across **continents**. The River Danube, for example, is one of Europe's longest rivers at 2,850 kilometres (1,770 miles). It begins in the Black Forest region of Germany, and flows from there through Austria, Slovakia, Hungary, Croatia, and Serbia and Montenegro. It then becomes the border between Romania and Bulgaria, crosses Romania and eventually ends in the Black Sea.

Mountains, rain, and rivers

The world's big mountain ranges are the starting points for many rivers. When rain falls on a mountain, it will collect and flow on either one side of the mountain or another. This means that the highest points along the mountain tops become the line that divides one river from the next. We call this line the **watershed**. Watersheds can be on any ground that is higher than the surrounding areas, not just in mountainous areas.

▼ This map shows some of the major rivers and mountain ranges of the world.

Rivers come and go

There are some parts of the world where there are no rivers marked on the map, for example in the desert areas of northern Africa. This is because the **climate** here is very dry, and sometimes years can pass without any rain. When rain does fall, it usually falls in very heavy storms. The rainstorms create rivers in the sand and across the dry rock. However, these rivers soon disappear when the rain stops. The sun beats down on them and the water dries up. After a short while only dry **river beds** remain.

Some areas of the world, for example southern Asia, have two main seasons during the year. One is dry and the other is wet. Rivers often flow only in the wet season, when there is a lot of rainfall. These are called **seasonal rivers**.

▼ Heavy rain in Algeria caused this dry river near Tamanrasset to suddenly flood with water.

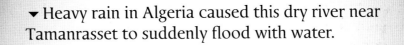

The river system

A **river system** is made up of one major river and all the streams and other rivers (**tributaries**) that flow into it. The total area of land that a river system drains is called its **drainage basin**, which is also known as a catchment area. A drainage basin is separated from other drainage basins by the high ground around it. This dividing ridge between drainage basins is the **watershed**.

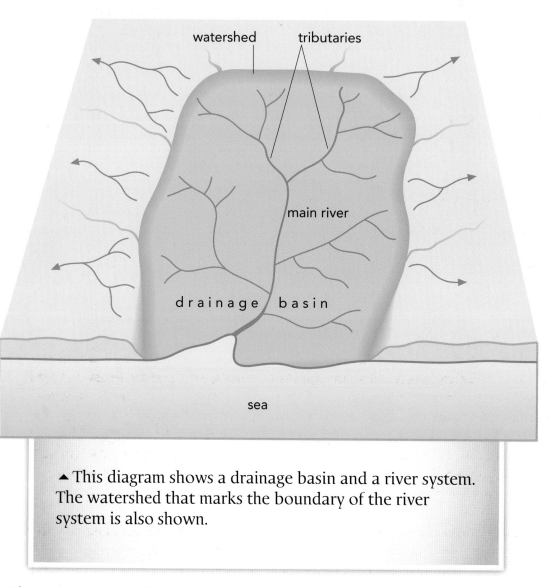

watershed   tributaries

main river

d r a i n a g e   b a s i n

sea

▲ This diagram shows a drainage basin and a river system. The watershed that marks the boundary of the river system is also shown.

The river system is the water that you can actually see flowing over the ground in rivers and streams. More water also feeds the river system from under the ground. When rain falls on land some of it soaks through the earth and soft rock.

◀ Water exists on Earth in many different forms. You can see some of them here: water, snow, ice, mist, and clouds. All of these forms of water are part of the water cycle.

Earth's water cycle

There is always the same amount of water on Earth, but it can exist in different forms. Most of Earth's water fills our oceans and seas, and is salty. **Fresh water** is contained in lakes and **glaciers**, or runs in rivers and streams. Sometimes water falls as rain, snow, and ice. Some of this water soaks into the ground. At other times water is held in tiny droplets in clouds, mist, and fog. Sometimes you cannot see water at all. When it is sunny, surface water **evaporates** into the air. It rises into the air as invisible **water vapour**. Plants also release water vapour into the air through holes in their leaves.

As the water vapour rises it cools and forms clouds. As the clouds move higher into the atmosphere, the water in them cools even more and becomes water droplets. These droplets fall as rain. The rain then fills streams, rivers, lakes, and seas. When the sun beats down on these waters, the same cycle begins again. This **water cycle** is also known as the hydrological cycle. It happens across the whole world, although some parts of the world are a lot wetter than others.

From the mountains to the sea

The start of a river is known as its **source**. The source can be mountain **springs**, where water bubbles up out of the ground and flows down a mountain's steep sides. It can also be small streams, formed by rainwater, that trickle over the steep rock. Some rivers begin as mountain marshes.

The water at the source of the river is pulled down the slope by Earth's **gravity**. It carries on, joined by other streams and rivers called **tributaries**, until it reaches a lake or the sea. This point is called the river's **mouth**. The journey between the source and the mouth is known as its **course**.

As the river flows along its course it carves out a **channel**. Gravity tries to pull the river down in a straight line, but the water finds all sorts of obstacles in its way. It is these obstacles that help make the curved shapes of our river landscapes.

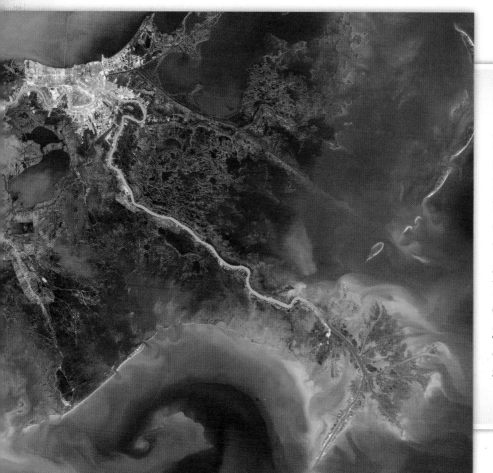

◄ When rivers carry large amounts of silt, such as the Mississippi River in the USA, it gets deposited as the river meets the sea. This creates landforms called **deltas**, which gradually build up as more and more silt is deposited.

Making the channel

Earth and rock are worn away as the river flows over them. This process is called **erosion**, and a process called **transportation** carries the eroded material away. The river water erodes some material, but the small bits of rock and soil carried in the water also wear some away. This rock and soil is called the river's **load**. The load bumps and scrapes along the channel, and wears it away. This kind of erosion is known as **corrasion**.

Rivers also carry chemicals in the water. Some of these chemicals dissolve soft rock. This type of erosion is called **corrosion**. A third type of erosion is **attrition**, which is when the rocks and stones on the **river bed** crash against each other. This breaks the rocks and stones into even smaller pieces – small enough to be carried away by the flowing water.

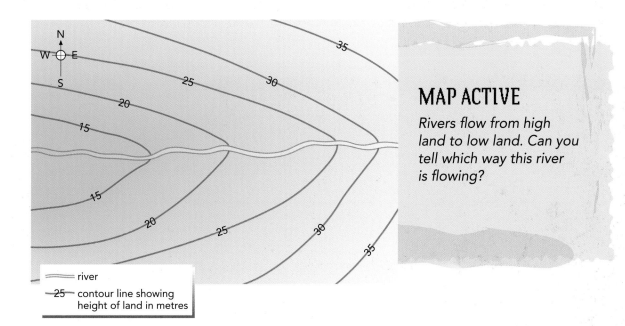

N
W — E
S

35
25
30
20
15
15
20
25
30
35

═══ river
—25— contour line showing height of land in metres

MAP ACTIVE

Rivers flow from high land to low land. Can you tell which way this river is flowing?

Changing the channel

Erosion and **deposition** change the shape and depth of the river's channel all the time. Deposition is when the river drops its load of rocks and soil. Deposition mostly occurs when there has been heavy rainfall because the river is full and flowing fast. Fast rivers can carry higher loads of eroded material, but as soon as the water slows it begins to drop its load. The river drops heavy rocks and boulders first, and then smaller stones. When the river reaches the sea it slows right down and deposits fine material called **silt**.

River landscapes

Rivers erode, transport, and deposit material all the time. They do this to help them find the easiest way to the sea.

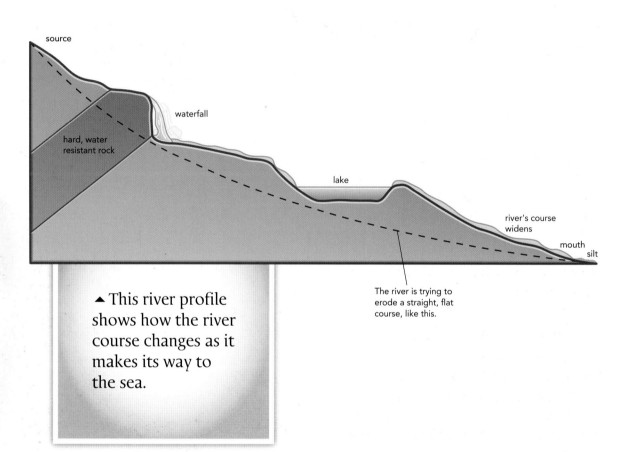

source

hard, water
resistant rock

waterfall

lake

river's course
widens

mouth

silt

The river is trying to
erode a straight, flat
course, like this.

▲ This river profile shows how the river course changes as it makes its way to the sea.

The river profile

The diagram above shows the **profile** (side view) of a river as it runs its **course**. The profile is not smooth and gradual. This is because the river has easily eroded the soft rock, but it takes much longer to wear away the hard rock. The river has to crash down over the edge of the hard rock as a waterfall. In some rivers there may be a lake to enter and leave before the water finally makes it to the sea.

The dotted line shows what the river is trying to do. It is trying to wear away a totally smooth profile. This would give the river an easy journey to its **mouth**.

Shapes in the course

As the river leaves the high ground it reaches the valley floor, which it has helped to carve out. Here it carves out its **channel** in the softest rock. Often the sides of the channel are more quickly worn than the bottom, so the river starts to wind back and forth along the valley floor.

Further along, the valley floor gets wider and flatter. This part is called the **flood plain**. As the river curves from side to side, the water on the inside of the curves moves more slowly than on the outside. The river begins to deposit **silt** here. This makes the water curve further and further out to the side, as it tries to get around these silt deposits. These curves are called **meanders**.

Where the river meets the sea

When the river joins the sea it flows very slowly, and its **load** of fine silt finally sinks. If the river is carrying very large amounts of silt it may be deposited to form a **delta**. The river will often divide into many channels called **distributaries** before finally making it into the sea. This area is usually very low-lying and easily floods.

▸ This river in Queensland, Australia, has large winding meanders as it makes its way through the valley floor.

The mighty Nile

The River Nile is the longest river in the world. It flows along the east side of Africa for 6,670 kilometres (4,140 miles). Its **source** springs from Lake Victoria in Uganda. The river flows from Lake Victoria northwards until it reaches Egypt and the Mediterranean Sea. The Nile has many distinct features all along its **course**. Some of these features are natural, but many are man-made, for example **dams**. The Nile flows through different types of **climate** and vegetation.

The course of the Nile

The river **profile** on page 12 shows a simple course. There is just one waterfall and one lake as the river makes its way to the sea. You can see from the map that the Nile has a long, complicated course. There are many **tributary** rivers, waterfalls, and lakes. There are long stretches of **turbulent** waters that run over huge boulders in the river **channel**. These stretches are called **cataracts**. The river flows into lakes and then out of them again. It passes through a great swamp known as the Sudd. The Nile has thousands of small **meanders**. It also has two huge bends that pass through the Nubian Desert. There are many dams on the river, which are used to control water levels. This is so people can operate boats and water their crops. Dams also provide electricity and drinking water.

◀ Many different types of boat sail along the wide, deep parts of the River Nile. These small trading vessels are called feluccas.

Different climates

The Nile is so long that it flows through areas of different climates. The river has a high, cool source in the mountains. It then passes through forests that are warm and wet until it reaches the **flood plain** where the climate is very hot and dry. At the coast there are cool, wet winters and hot, dry summers, which is known as a Mediterranean climate. The River Nile is very important for **irrigation** in the dry areas near to the **mouth** of the river.

◀ The course of the River Nile as it makes its way from Lake Victoria to the Mediterranean Sea.

MAP ACTIVE
Describe where dams are found along the Nile.

River plants

Where river plants grow

Flowing water provides a good **habitat** for both plants and animals. Many plants have **adapted** well to living in it. However, near the **source** of rivers many plants do not grow well. These shallow, fast-flowing stretches of rivers have stony beds that make it hard for plants to take root. Here, mosses and tiny **algae** grow best because they can hug the rocks.

▼ The bulrush is also known as reed mace or cattail. It grows in shallow **fresh water** in many parts of the world. Bulrushes grow up to about 2.5 metres (8 feet) tall. The stems and leaves of the bulrush are used to make ropes, mats, and baskets.

Algae are the simplest form of plant life. They have a jelly-like coating that reduces the rubbing action (friction) of the flowing water. Small mosses cling on with grips that grow in line with the flowing **current**. This stops the water from pressing hard against them and tearing the mosses away from the rocks. On the **flood plain** the river bed often has fine, deep, rich soil – as do the marshes that spread out from the river. Here, many larger plants have been able to adapt to life in and around the water. These larger plants help to provide oxygen for the animals that live in the river.

▲ The water hyacinth comes from South America, but has spread to other parts of the world. The leaf stalks have air pockets that help the plant to float well above the surface. The water hyacinth is sometimes known as the 'million-dollar weed'. This is because it has cost millions of dollars to stop it from clogging up rivers in the southern United States!

River animals

Rivers teem with many kinds of **mammals**, **amphibians**, **reptiles**, birds, fish, and **invertebrates**. Most animals live in the calmer waters of the **flood plain** and marshlands. Others have **adapted** to living in the fast-flowing waters higher up the river's **course**. They have developed streamlined bodies that reduce the impact of the rushing water. The larvae of blackfly spin a pad of silk on to a rock that they then hold on to firmly with hooks.

▲ What is this amazing creature with a duck's bill, webbed feet, a furry body, and a squashed tail? It is a mammal called a duck-billed platypus. The platypus lives in southern Australia, and Tasmania. The female digs burrows in the riverbank and, unlike most mammals, she lays eggs. The platypus uses its flat tail and webbed feet to swim. The long and very sensitive bill stirs up the mud at the bottom of the river. This uncovers the platypus's food of insects, worms, and shellfish.

Living in the river

Most animals that live in the water need to be able to move around and have adaptations to help them do this. Mammals such as beavers, amphibians such as frogs, and waterbirds such as ducks have developed webbed feet. Crocodiles are reptiles that swim by using their long powerful tails. Reptiles stay in the water for a long time, but come up to the surface to breathe air. River mammals can also hold their breath for a long time underwater. This is so that they can find their food.

◄ The Atlantic salmon lives in parts of the Atlantic Ocean until it is time to breed. Then it swims upriver, leaping up fast-flowing sections using its strong muscles. The female lays thousands of eggs. The adult fish then let the river **current** take them back down to the sea. The young salmon hatch and stay in the river for about two years. Then they go down to the sea until it is time for them to breed.

Amphibians take in the oxygen dissolved in the water through their skin. The skin is thin, with a lot of blood vessels near the surface. This is so that oxygen gets taken into the bloodstream very quickly. They can also breathe when they are out of the water. Fish use **gills** at the sides of their heads to get oxygen from the water.

Some very large animals can live in rivers. In some African countries, hippopotamuses spend most of their time wallowing in rivers. This is because they need to stay cool and prevent their skin being burned by the sun. They usually come out of the river at night to graze on the vegetation growing along the sides of the river.

Living with the river

For thousands of years rivers have provided humans with drinking water, food, and well-watered farmland. Riverside plants have been used as materials for building homes both in and around the water.

Boats have been made from river reeds, wood, and tree bark. Rivers have given people a way of transporting goods and people to other settlements.

Rivers have protected people against their enemies. Many old towns and villages were built where a **tributary** joins the main river. This provided even better protection because the settlement had rivers running up two sides. Some ancient settlements were built inside the loop of a **meander**. This meant that only one wall needed to be built to protect the community. Many rivers also provide a natural border between countries, such as the Rio Grande which marks the border between the United States and Mexico. Rivers are so important to the world that they have become part of religion for many people.

Rivers can also bring problems for settlements, however, such as flooding. Diseases, such as malaria, are also more widespread near wet or damp areas.

▼ Steamboats helped the river port of New Orleans to grow in southern USA. This great city curves around a bend in a wide part of the Mississippi River. Ships can sail from here to the Atlantic Ocean along channels that have been **dredged** to make them deeper.

Cities and civilizations

Some of the greatest cities of the world began as small settlements built where rivers flow deep and wide. Large boats brought goods and people here. This allowed trade to develop. Later, factories were built in cities near the river. Factory owners used **raw materials**, such as cotton, brought by ships. The raw materials were then manufactured into goods.

Great civilizations also developed on the banks of rivers. Ancient Egypt grew around the banks of the River Nile around 5,000 years ago.

▼ Map of a large meander in a river and some contour lines to show the height of the surrounding land.

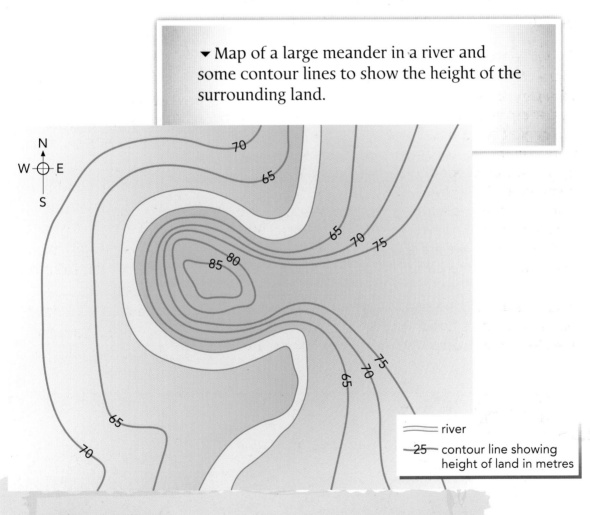

river

25 — contour line showing height of land in metres

MAP ACTIVE

If you were building an ancient settlement, where could you locate the following: a castle, a defensive wall, a bridge, and farmland?

A way of life – Bangladesh

Most of Bangladesh lies where the great Ganges and Brahmaputra Rivers meet and flow into the Indian Ocean. In this **delta** area, the land is very flat and low-lying. During the cool, dry months the rivers fork out into **distributaries**. These make their way out into the Indian Ocean. During the summer months rain pours down and water flows from the melting snows in the great Himalayan mountain range.

The river delta becomes flooded with water that covers many square kilometres. Sometimes high sea tides caused by very bad weather, called storm surges, create huge waves that smother the delta in seawater. The floodwaters kill many of the plants beneath them, but billions of tiny blue-green **algae** feed on these dead plants and create lots of nitrogen in the soil. This makes the land very **fertile** and good for farming.

▼ The areas of Bangladesh most at risk of flooding. The land most at risk is low-lying and either next to one of the rivers or close to the sea.

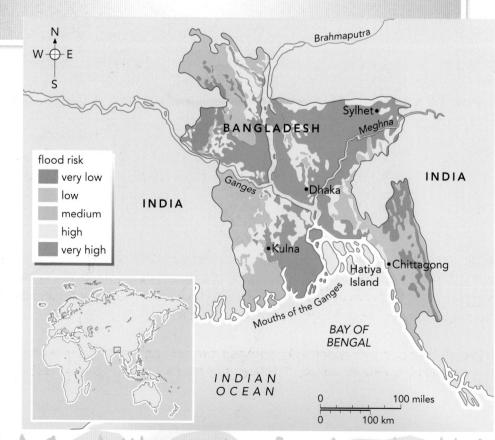

Living and working in Bangladesh

The people living on the delta always have to be prepared for flooding. They build their homes on banks or platforms of earth between the river **channels**. Most of the houses are made of wood and are raised on stilts. Even so, flooding often causes a lot of deaths and damage to farmland.

In the dry winters the ground is full of large holes. This is where the earth was dug up to make the banks and platforms. The holes are called borrow pits. Water fills the pits and is used for drinking and washing. It is also used for **irrigating** crops.

▲ Jute is grown in Bangladesh where the farmland floods. Its stems are woody and have many fibres. These are soaked, dried, and made into rope, sacking, and matting.

Most people in Bangladesh are farmers. Two or three crops of rice are grown every year in the rich, damp soil. **Tropical** fruits, beans, oilseeds, wheat, vegetables, bamboo, and jute are also grown. Nearly a million tonnes of fish are caught every year. Most are freshwater fish.

A lot of the country's electricity comes from oil and coal-fired power stations, but some comes from water. This is called **hydroelectric power (HEP)**.

Our changing rivers

Rivers change naturally all the time, but the way humans use rivers also changes them.

Natural flooding?

Flooding happens all the time, and it is a natural process. It occurs when there is a lot of melting snow and ice or when there is very heavy rainfall. After a flood the river **channel** may have changed because there has been a lot of **erosion** and **deposition** of material in the river.

Over the last few years flooding has increased. One of the worst floods was on the River Yangtze in China, in 1998. Many people lost their lives and homes. What has made the floods so bad? People are partly to blame.

▼ The waterwheel is an ancient form of irrigation. This one in southern Germany picks up water in the buckets and tips it into the wooden channel, which leads to the fields.

Taking the water – changing the flow

Humans have made some of the greatest changes to rivers. One of the most important has been building **dams**. Dams are often built on rivers to store water and to direct it on to dry farmland for **irrigation**. Some irrigation systems use water straight from the river. This changes the way the river erodes its channel and deposits material.

Thousands of years ago, river irrigation was used in ancient Egypt, China, and Peru. Early Native Americans irrigated more than 1,000 square kilometres (386 square miles) of land in Arizona's Salt River valley.

◀ The Riano reservoir in Spain was made to irrigate farmland and to provide power. The old town of Riano had to be moved from the **fertile** valley floor to the bare mountainside because the dam meant that the valley was flooded.

Changing times

Today, boats can sail from the Atlantic Ocean up the River Guadalquivir to the city of Seville in Spain. This is a distance of 80 kilometres (50 miles). Long ago, boats were able to reach the city port of Cordoba, a further 100 kilometres (75 miles) beyond Seville. Over time, the river channel filled with **silt**. This silting has created the Donana marshlands, which are now home to many types of marshland birds and animals.

Looking to the future

Dam building, flooding, and pollution are upsetting **river systems** throughout the world. Most of these problems are made by humans. We use too much water in our homes and industry – and too much energy. We pollute the rain and the rivers. The future of our rivers depends on us.

The problem of dams

Dams have been built for **irrigation** and to help rivers flow all year round. They also provide **hydroelectric power (HEP)**. The cascading water let out through the dam wall turns **turbines** that provide electricity.

Dams can flood villages and river landscapes when they are built and start to fill up. They affect the natural flow of rivers and can dry up river systems and destroy the **habitats** of river wildlife.

Flooding

Floods kill people and destroy homes and farmland. They also alter river **channels** and systems. Floods have become worse in recent years. This is partly because storms have become more frequent and more violent. Many scientists blame this on the world's slightly hotter weather. The increased heat **evaporates** more moisture, which turns into more rain clouds.

Some scientists think the hotter weather is caused by too many harmful gases going up into the atmosphere. These have thinned the layer of ozone gases that protects us from the Sun's heat. Other harmful gases may also be responsible for hotter weather. Carbon dioxide is released when we burn fossil fuels (coal, oil, and gas). The carbon dioxide rises into the atmosphere and traps Earth's heat inside. This is called the greenhouse effect. All these things disrupt the **water cycle**, which means that our rivers are also affected.

▲ Polluting rivers with chemicals harms the river habitat. Chemicals from factories kill river plants. River plants put oxygen into the water. Fish need this oxygen to breathe, so they can also be affected.

River facts

Ten longest rivers

These are the 10 longest rivers of the world. Some of them run through more than one country, but only the country where the river mostly runs through is named.

River	Continent	Country	Length
Nile	Africa	Egypt	6,670 kilometres (4,140 miles)
Amazon	South America	Brazil	6,450 kilometres (4,010 miles)
Yangtze	Asia	China	6,380 kilometres (3,960 miles)
Mississippi-Missouri	North America	USA	6,020 kilometres (3,740 miles)
Yenisey-Angara	Asia	Russia	5,550 kilometres (3,445 miles)
Hwang Ho	Asia	China	5,464 kilometres (3,395 miles)
Ob-Irtysh	Asia	Russia	5,410 kilometres (3,360 miles)
Congo	Africa	Democratic Republic of Congo	4,670 kilometres (2,900 miles)
Mekong	Asia	China	4,500 kilometres (2,795 miles)
Parana-Plate	South America	Paraguay	4,500 kilometres (2,795 miles)

... and the shortest

- The shortest river with a name is the Roe River in Montana, USA. It is only 61 metres (200 feet) long!
- Did you know that the Mississippi **Delta** is expanding every year by about 100 metres (328 feet)?

Polluted rivers

- The Cuyahoga River in Ohio, USA, became so polluted that it caught fire several times between 1936 and 1969! Since then, great efforts have been made to clean up our polluted rivers.
- The River Ganges in India and Bangladesh is a holy river for followers of the Hindu religion. Many people bathe in the waters at sunrise. This is part of their daily prayer. When a person dies their ashes, and flowers, are sprinkled on the river.

Find out more

Further reading

Earth Files: Rivers and Lakes, Chris Oxlade (Heinemann Library, 2002)
Horrible Geography: Raging Rivers, Anita Ganeri (Scholastic, 2005)
Landscapes and People: Earth's Changing Rivers, Neil Morris (Raintree, 2003)
Our World: Rivers and Lakes, Kate Bedford (Hodder Wayland, 2005)
Step Up Geography: Investigating Rivers, Clare Hibbert (Evans Brothers, 2005)

Websites

www.associationofriverstrusts.org.uk/
The website of the Association of Rivers Trusts, which represents river trusts in England and Wales and promotes solutions to environmental issues.

www.bbc.co.uk/nature/animals/wildbritain/habitats/freshwater/
Find out about the natural life in freshwater streams and rivers in the UK.

www.geography.learnontheinternet.co.uk/topics/river.html
Factual information about rivers, with case studies to support topics covered.

Map Active answers

Page 11: This river is flowing from east to west. We can tell because the higher ground is to the east and the lower ground is to the west. Rivers always flow downhill due to **gravity**, so this river must flow from east (high ground) to west (low ground).

Page 15: There are many **dams** on the Nile. There is one just after the river leaves its **source**, Lake Victoria. The next one on this river, the White Nile, is just before Khartoum. There are two dams on the Blue Nile between its source (Lake Tana) and Khartoum, where it joins the White Nile. The Nile has one further dam between Lake Nasser and Aswan.

Page 21: These are excellent places to locate the following:
- Castle – the best place is on the high ground on the inside of the **meander** loop. This means that on three sides of the castle, enemies would have to cross the river and climb a steep hill in order to mount an attack.
- Defensive wall – this would be best built on the eastern side of the castle, where the land is flat and there is no river to cross.
- Bridge – the best place would be where the river narrows, south of the meander loop. The land is also quite flat on either side of the river here.
- Farmland – the best place is on the flat land on the western side of the river, because the soil will be **fertile** here and the flat land will be easy to manage.

Glossary

adapt change to suit certain environmental conditions

algae simple form of plant life

amphibian animal that develops in water and can stay in the water for long periods, but can also live on land

attrition erosion caused by friction or gradual wearing away

cataract waterfall or series of waterfalls

channel passage in the ground where water collects and flows

climate rainfall, temperature, and winds that affect a large area over a long period of time

continent any one of the world's largest continuous land masses

corrasion when stones get carried along by flowing water and bump against the river's bed and sides, eroding them away

corrosion when something is gradually eaten away, for example through being dissolved by chemicals

course journey of a river between its source and its mouth

current water that flows constantly in one direction

dam wall that is built across a river valley to hold back water, creating an artificial lake behind it

delta flat area of land created by a river depositing material as it enters an ocean, sea, or lake

deposition when a river drops its load of rock and silt on the river bed

distributary one of the streams a river separates into when it reaches its delta

drainage basin basin-shaped area of Earth, surrounded by a watershed, in which a river and its tributaries flow

dredge dig out layers of silt on a river bed

erosion wearing away of rocks and soil by wind, water, ice, or chemicals

evaporate turn from solid or liquid into vapour, such as when water becomes water vapour

fertile rich soil in which crops can grow easily

flood plain flat land in a valley bottom that is regularly flooded

fresh water water that is not salty like the sea

gill organ on animals living in water which takes in oxygen from the water

glacier huge river of ice and compressed snow that flows slowly down a mountain

gravity force that causes all objects to be pulled towards Earth

habitat place where a plant or animal usually grows or lives

hydroelectric power (HEP) electricity produced by the power of falling water

invertebrate animal without a backbone

irrigation supplying a place or area with water, for example to grow crops

load material carried by a river

mammal animal that feeds its young with its own milk

meander large bend in a river's course

mouth place where a river meets the sea

profile side view

raw materials natural materials that can be made into other things

reptile cold-blooded, egg-laying animal with a spine and scaly skin, such as a crocodile

river bed the bottom of a river channel

river system river and all the streams (tributaries) that run into it

seasonal river river that only flows when there is a lot of rainfall

silt fine particles of eroded rock and soil that can settle in lakes and rivers, sometimes blocking the movement of water

source where a river begins

spring source of river where water bubbles up out of the ground

transportation process by which pieces of earth and rock are carried away by water

tributary stream or river that runs into a main river

tropical hot and humid area around the middle of Earth

turbine revolving motor that is pushed around by water or steam and can produce electricity

turbulent strong and wild

water cycle movement of water between the air, land, and sea

watershed high land that separates neighbouring drainage basins

water vapour water that has been heated so much that it forms a gas that is held in the air

Index